The Lighted Pull of Dreams

poems by

Abby Lynn Bogomolny

Finishing Line Press
Georgetown, Kentucky

The Lighted Pull of Dreams

ACKNOWLEDGMENTS

"A Clutch and a Spin" in a different version in *Nauseous in Paradise*

"I Said to Poetry" in a different version in *Stolen Light: 2016 Redwood
Writers Poetry Anthology*

"Mother Left in January" under another title and different version in *Vintage
Voices: The Sound of a Thousand Leaves*

"On Leaving" appeared in *Stolen Light: 2016 Redwood Writers Poetry
Anthology*

"Swept" under another name and version in *Nauseous in Paradise*

"The Blue Green Jewel Her Body" in a different version in *Black of Moonlit
Sea; in People Who Do Not Exist*; in *Water: Redwood Writers Anthology*; and
*The Freedom of New Beginnings: Poems of Witness and Vision from Sonoma
County Writers*

"The Bus Station" in *Fighting Words: 25 Years of Provocative Poetry and Prose
from the "Blue Collar PEN*;" and in *And the Beats Go On: Redwood Writers
Poetry Anthology*

"The Lighted Pull of Dreams" in another version and title in *Black of Moonlit
Sea*; and in another version in *In the Light of Peace*

"The Lightless Hour" in another version in *Black of Moonlit Sea*; and in
People Who Do Not Exist

Publisher: Leah Huete de Maines
Editor: Christen Kincaid
Cover Art: Abby Lynn Bogomolny
Author Photo: Abby Lynn Bogomolny
Cover Design: Elizabeth Maines McCleavy

Order online: www.finishinglinepress.com
also available on amazon.com

Author inquiries and mail orders:
Finishing Line Press
PO Box 1626
Georgetown, Kentucky 40324
USA

Contents

In Memory of Frances and Samuel Bogomolny

The Lighted Pull of Dreams

inky black moonlit sea
our walk at midnight
by the lighthouse

bundled warm from the cold
after a dim day of rain
in housebound January

other nights I fly
over the hill
where mist lingers
in silver patches

breathe
the airbourne fog

on the return
a fringe of redwood fingers
brushes my gleaming belly

outstretched wings glide me
I am pulled by the sureness
of gravity
and my love
of returning to you

with the turning
earth, so do we
half in waking   the other
half, sleep
we fall inside
and retreat

as green things twist
an inch
daily
towards the sun,
we drift closer

invisible to eyes outside
we fall and fly
flapping and feeding
we flock like seagulls
to the lighted pull of dreams

Their Silver Allure

"What's Montague? It is nor hand, nor foot/ Nor arm, nor face."
—William Shakespeare, Romeo & Juliet, Act II, Scene II

Montague Street meets the Brooklyn Heights Promenade,
overlooking the East River where new lovers
take euphoria out for a stroll, pillow creases
on their faces, they gaze at the skyline
of lower Manhattan, seeing luxury suites,
boxy high rises, and the squashed windows
of projects—oh the brick of it,
the pothole of it, what happens to dreams,
when does forever hit a narrow wall,
the lives of our parents
and our parent's parents
walking institutional hallways
or on deathbeds
distant scratchy voices on phone lines
running from or to our promises—
our ever-elusive, shivering dreams,
their silver allure sings to us:

Seven miles away from Brooklyn Heights,
my father made a promise in a house with a sandstone stoop,
and a wrought iron door that led to the vestibule that opened
to a cool, dark hallway with the smells of old country cooking.
A house where kids charged the alley to a courtyard to play ball
against brick, three stories high, a house with wine jugs
and coal bins in the basement where the boiler was fed
and meters read, house of my father's power tunneling
to his youth, plants on the fire escapes as they rose to the roof.
A time when refugee neighbors pronounced our name like a melody
and savored the rolling rise of it, meaning "one who prays to God,"
a name said with care, not an obstacle
that challenged clumsy mouths.

The house, a dream of my grandparents,
one my grandmother chose, not by the fire station,
or under the El, away from sirens and rattling after years
of saving, selling children's clothes from a pushcart,
after years of sweating in their laundry.
A three-story attached walkup of sand-colored brick,
with six two-bedroom apartments. A house where for a time,
my grandparents, my father, his two sisters, the married sister's husband
and their new baby lived in one apartment until my aunt and uncle
moved downstairs, welcomed a second child, and a dog named Trudy.

A house from which I stared out a north-facing window
to the courtyard as a little girl—years later,
without brothers and sisters, and grandparents gone,
I heard the conversations embedded
in the wallpaper. Russia had left sharp stones
in my grandparents' shoes. Hidden compartments
in the closet walls and desks with false bottoms.
My aunt said that my father once brought home
his high school trophy for winning the 100-yard dash,
but my grandmother stared at him. Instead of a smile
and congratulations, she slapped him across the face:
"Any dope can win a race," she said, "I want you to study
and become somebody."

Oh the narrow wall of it. The freezing rain breaks
granite and schist, cracks concrete and asphalt.
Salt sprinkled on the roads melts ice and snow, but eats
steel and chrome. I asked father why the trunk handle
of our old car was covered with bumps, the trunk
someone jimmyed and stole his box of shoe samples,
all for the right foot.

Lost an Hour Today

looked for it
in the refrigerator,
under the couch,
cracks in floor,
but still no hour.
       maybe time
       tripped when I turned
       off the car key
       and sat staring
       ahead, inhaling silence,
       or maybe time dropped
       as I carried bags
       to my door
so I searched—
found one carrot
and a thin line of flour
down the walkway to the porch
little hole in bag, still no hour,
time wears me out.
       when the alarm split open my dream,
       the clock read 5:30, but I knew it was 4:30,
       k n e w the angle of sun, k n e w the whir
       of hummingbirds frantic and diving
       for their turn at the feeder.
time may be trying
to hitch a ride out of here
because men decided to borrow a spring hour.
frantic, we drop off our best moments
at the coat check of deliberation,
promising to return an hour in the fall,
sand moves silently through the hourglass
dead-end jobs steal years.
       time could be standing
       with her thumb out near the on-ramp
       to the freeway,
       what will we do without her?

July Joy: 1775

everyone
loves my husband,
but I married him for his sister.
we tend the garden together
as our strength and youth are equals.
most long and dusty mornings
we move in harmony,
through the rows
lilt and limb,
step and lift,
her long wavy hair tied,
until a need draws us to the creek
whereupon we splash, laugh, and float
as her hair, a freshwater fan,
envelopes me in its lively joy.

my mother knows
as she prepares meals at our hearth
that my husband labors far from here
to earn the land that feeds the family,
and as a son of liberty, he will be
the first to fight for the colonies.

I suppose he is kind, compared to most men,
who swear, drink, and treat us roughly.
every few months he returns for a spell
during which he hopes to leave me with child.
while it's not proper to speak of such,
his sister never leaves me weak or sore.
if I do not look forward to this chore,
it is not that I am ungrateful:
we would not have this home without him,
but without his sister,
there would be no joy.

The Lightless Hour

maybe it is the lightless hour
that allows us to drift
  freely this way
      the night without edges
         in moonlight is before us
we can escape like smoke
      through the window.

let us go
let us go
in only a few minutes
  they may come for us.

Events May Send One

down the chute narrow of metallic cold
whose sides close in
as it tunnels below
to be spat into a sap-sucking slot
a cement corridor dimly lit.
a jagged space in which to stretch,
breathe and pull ourselves to sleep.
deprivation spawns habits that gnaw
at our core till we scream
at others not to weep.

Saved

You're still cute as sweet potato pie, grey bangs falling over brown brows, eyes alive and bright with a *can do*-wide grin of still-perfect teeth. Years ago you plucked me off the molten July streets of Manhattan and offered me shelter in a red farm house on a Florida hill. Orange grove on one side, pecan grove on the other, behind it a gentle slope through a field, dotted with grazing horses to the fresh water of the little lake. You were 35 that first day I landed. I saw flip flops flapping at the end of your strong brown legs, saw two long brown braids that framed your grin as I hopped into your Corolla. You became my unofficial official manager, protector, and model star-gazing poet writing a dissertation about the astrological influences bubbling through Henry David Thoreau's *Walden*. Your work written from the 2nd floor upstairs view of the fields, orchards, and sky full of poetry. Introduced me to doodle bugs in the grass, red bugs in the Spanish moss, flying Palmetto bugs you'd catch in paper bags. How to use nail polish to paint over a bad case of chiggers, and A200 when some stranger sat in the living room in a damp bathing suit which allowed lice to migrate…cause that's all it took. Your mom a high school English teacher in Baton Rouge. Drew me down to the lake we shared with cows to which you paid no mind, but complained about the fertilizer seeping down that encouraged algae. Pulled me slow with your car down the road on roller skates. You wrung a lot of vowels out of each word. Let me bring my no-good girlfriend down on Amtrak who traveled with a paper bag of underwear, a Vodka bottle, and her trumpet. Took me to Palatka for food stamps. Told me to stay out of the kitchen and off the phone in lightning storms. Found me gigs as the acoustic singer-songwriter to draw gaggles of gals to the bar. Mabel's Blue Water Bay; Gainesville's Bilbo and Gandalf's, Monk's Inn; Jacksonville's Little Dude, and St. Augustine's Pagoda. Let me decorate the ground floor bathroom with palm fronds stapled to the walls. In the orange-blossomed springtime, I learned what it was like to live inside a perfume bottle. Every day one of plenty. Your theatre named The Frothing Slosh and your land down the road. Each week you held court in the living room with a jug of wine and a ring of women, one of which your current flame as your steady girlfriend slept upstairs. I was 21 and planned to stay two weeks. Stayed 10 years.

Swept

Even the sweat of July could not stop us:
the windless, stifling afternoon, fraught
with a white-hot sun and teabag humidity.
In a quiet, nowhere-little town, fevered
baked and soggy, we were close, water
oozing from our pores, indoors
with the fan blowing, or outdoors
in the porcelain bathtub beneath giant pecans,
spiraling lianas, and green lush life,
awaiting four o'clock rain.

Later under the crescent moon, you pointed
to the Pleiades on St George island.
Nothing could stop us from going camping
in my pickup, off the Florida panhandle.
The muggy pine flats were deserted
as were the wide, soft beaches
swept into dunes by gulf winds
that made sand fleas burrow.
For eight sweaty miles we hiked, hauling
our water to the bay side of the island
where the only well belched a sulfurous brine.

When the sun dipped low and long wispy clouds
went wild in a display, resembling the color of salmon,
golden jewels, and the purple of pokeberries,
ospreys and pelicans dove down to the same liquid
dinner table. Above an oyster reef,
we stood in the brisk bay wind that dried the sweat
and kept the mosquitoes from a feeding frenzy
with us on the menu. Your eyes followed gull-billed
terns while I painted swirling pastel clouds,
and we sighed with contentment as folks
from Alabama dropped down the map to twang
and sip beer on vacation. We were real good then.

The Blue Green Jewel Her Body

there's a river of light on the highway, they want to go home
they don't eat their dinner with family, they eat alone
to someone
to someone   somewhere
another woman in a compact car
hears the low cry, wound to her middle bleeding

thousands of parking lots   thousands of cars
choke on themselves, roads twist   snakelike,
a skin of tar, stretched tightly,   crumbles

even her house is on wheels, piled backseat high
food, papers, shoes   everyone burns
everyone burns, burns
slime   from deep searing holes,

The blue green jewel her body
to anyone
to anyone   anywhere
do you feel the central cry?
do we continue to trade the green sweetness?
highways swathed over the wounds
to her middle bleeding
there's a river of light on the highway, they want to go home
they don't eat their dinner with family, they eat alone

On Leaving

Here is the branch she stepped on; then complained it was bent.
Here is the mare she tried riding up steep hills.
In this land of the parched, there is no tender grass.

Any four-legged knows the difference between friend and foe,
but people abandon horse sense. They wrangle reasons,
and weave a bitter fabric of regret.
Do not waste your time.
Any mare will turn toward kindness;
she will know how to protect her big heart
or run from a damaged hut.
Please leave at once; do not linger when starving.

Young Moon

She rose in east of evening, ghostlike and pale
Across from a mandarin sunset of fire
Her thin curves concerned me, kept me mired
On her safety, moving lonely and frail.
In a universe of danger and asteroids,
I willed the use of my thick black wings
For her blanket and warmth, the faded thing
Though the sky's dim light left me compromised.
I stationed myself above the cooling earth
As her rise flew far above my perch,
Unheard and unseen by bear, bat, or lark
Her wedge of light daggered the dark.
How mistaken I was before to think her less
See how she beams, bright and strong in her crest.

The Bus Station

When my students stare up at me, restless with my lesson
or with outright pity for my clothing, I worry and wonder
where they will go and how they will fare—

My classroom feels like a bus station:
to the west is the freeway—in line of sight to the distant city
that casts off commuters and refugees.
one student arrives with a deformed child in his chest
another will be late,
missing a shoe, an ear, a father.
he will try to listen,
but has already taken too many orders
from his manager at the drug store.
another student will fold last week's pink slip
in her wallet, next to the photo of her teenaged daughter.
she will sit in her bus station classroom,
next to a skinny, tattooed boy out of high school,
feeling free for the first time to think and have opinions,
no longer a crinkled woman folding
sweaters all day at Macy's.

At this bus station,
they keep cutting the schedule
and issue tickets to uncertainty.
long lines form for limited seats,
at a time when the roadways are littered
with throwaways and distractions:
my classroom bears the burden.

In the Classroom

not a day of thunderous sneezes,
as textbooks fall to floors with a smack,
or blank faces conceal texting on laps,
and coffee mugs spill
on backpacks.
maybe Oscar will trip,
and Jessica will look away,
but it does not mean anything.
except Rick can not concentrate;
he broke his wrist in 9th grade,
and it aches when he presses into it.
Lucy proclaims her paragraph is terrible;
she hates to write without a laptop.
she crumples up her paper
just as Denise finishes her freewrite,
sweeping an arc across her desk into the air,
hitting Alejandro in the nose.
she's soooo embarrassed,
but not as upset as James,
who just remembered
we had homework due.

• • •

I long for those rare moments
when the only sounds are papers turning,
students engaged in holy work,
the brush of pencil lead across paper,
the click of keyboards,
the groan of chairs under shifting weight,
and I bathe in this silence,
admire their imaginations,
the pointed power of focused minds,
perhaps a small sneeze or soft cough,
will bring me back
from feeling that these efforts

will launch their best selves
like rockets, full of fiery beauty,
luck and grace
into the electric air
of their futures.

A Clutch and a Spin

You held your flared hats in place
with long hatpins; should fellows
with roving hands edge too close
in a packed elevator or subway,
you "gave them a little poke."

In dresses no longer
than the middle of your knee,
you played the hardy, stubborn
dame in sheer stockings,
who taught me the freshest
peppers were at the back of the bin.

When I was a child, you tugged
at my crotch in department stores
to judge the fit of my trousers.
With a mother's vengeance
you argued with sales clerks,
principals and garbage men.

My teen years were loud as a battle zone
my attitude met your hot flashes,
and we flared, searing pots and pans,
slamming cabinets, our screaming duets
by the kitchen window entertained
the whole apartment house.

So I am not surprised that you,
a determined woman in your 70s
on her way to the doctor's office
held on to her purse straps
with a strong clutch
and a surprising spin
that made a young, running
mugger give up his grip.

Pandemic Moon Sonnet

I rarely visit your embassy of care
With eyes cast down at shiny squares of chroma
When you rise and set is no longer clear
In the valley of a dark moon, Sonoma.
I so believe the hubris of my screen
Alone I sip time stolen by a thief
Who hands me weight of hard and heavy means,
In moods that measure not the length of grief.
I look outside and feel your cool bone shine,
The darkly bright reflections of our star,
A soothing light without the burn and find
A visa home where hopes awaiting are.
On long dark nights when nothing yet is certain
I see us dancing when they open up the curtain.

Mother Left in January

With the late light of winter as the sun
faded, you chose to leave this world, falling
beyond the sea to the west of Ocean Beach,
the sandy dunes and wide boulevards
of Sunset, San Francisco.

I, frantic daughter, watched your fire
fizzle and withdraw, essence only those
who felt your love full upon them knew
before thinning clouds of worry darkened.

I believed I could keep you in this world,
but your breath labored under liquid
and you fought, square feet on earth,
planted with each wheeze
for you, or me, I didn't know, until I said
"Wouldn't you rather be doing something else?"
and you smiled,
"It's ok Mom, go ahead, you can let go;
there's much to heal on the other side."

Then I gasped, hoping you knew
I did not want you to disappear,
but your warmth united, swept
a dance on the only stage in spotlight
of rainbow carrier for you, Frances,
lovely lady, in passage to mission of soul.

Outside the traffic still moved on Silver Avenue,
nurses wheeled their bedtime carts
to each room of the good home;
drawers opened and closed, cedar branches
shook in the wind, a small square of glass
on the wall held fading light,
the room grew hot from your emanation
needing to sign your name one more time.

We are of this world and yet another
in this room see proof—the sweat on my neck,
the hair on my arms drawn up in cosmic wind;
telepathy says it best, love's deep knowing
though we danced far too seriously—
stubborn, scolding, careful mother
rebellious, quiet, quirky daughter—
the cord of memory is clear, an unguarded love
swept together by the sun's withdrawing
speed of light and I am proud you are on your way.

Of the Light

We live in someone else's house
wide doors and window screens
though we hurl ourselves against the light
escape's beyond our means.

From the wide cave of her belly we came
to forage fruits of the sun
till strength moves us to challenge the night
with tremulous deeds of our own.

When fog fills the bowl of the bay
to later disperse on the roam,
we glance up as small diamonds of light
pour through her felt-covered dome.

Still living in someone else's house
wide doors and window screens,
we hurl ourselves against the light
with hope delivered by dreams.

From the wide bowl of her belly we came
to ripen with just enough glow
till it's time to trace our light show home
when we become what we came here to know.

At Your Age, Darling

My mother—may she rest in peace—spoke to me very plainly
yesterday, right before I called to book the belly dancer
for my party:

> *At your age, darling, anyone with sense would stop*
> *celebrating her birthday.*

Really?

> *You should care more about what people think.*

There's always something to celebrate, birthday or not.

> *You're impossible. I don't know why I keep talking to you.*

You can't help it. We're different, and it's another decade.

> *Some things remain the same.*

Yes, like wanting to see my friends.

> *You may not be ready to hear it, but some of your girlfriends*
> *are not your "friends." You call them exes.*

They're my family, Mom.

> *You would have been happier if you'd given the other side a chance.*

Won't you ever stop?

> *Well tell them not to bring you any more gifts;*
> *your house is full of dust collectors.*

I've asked them to bring side dishes and desserts.

Be sure to bake a chicken. And clean your house! You never finished the path through the yard; it's still a mess.

How do you know all this?

I'm magic.

All right, I'll weed the backyard and even put in a few slate tiles on the path.

Good. So I'm not invited?

You're always invited. Just don't scare anyone!

I Said to Poetry

Shut up!
Why do you choose
the exact moment I carry heavy
dishes of spaghetti to speak to me?
Why do you roll
out waves of words
when my best friend Phyllis
needs undivided attention?

Poetry, each time you lift me
like a party balloon, it takes
me hours to find balance.
When you transport me to planets
that swirl magnetic seas
of unbelievable colors,
how can you expect
me to remember
a counseling appointment?
No more of your distractions;
I have to live here.

Who are you, Poetry? And why
am I never sure when you'll arrive?
but when you do, you speak and I must
turn off the oven, turn off the electric
drill, lest casseroles turn crispy dark
and bookshelves enjoy their tilt.

Poetry, when the ceiling fan in my bathroom
conducts a radio station only I can hear,
how can I not absorb your music—your language?
No wonder people roll their eyes
at me. Far in the distance behind the fan
motor's whirl is a continuous melody,
a crystal temple's curl of harmonies,
overtones of eternal mystery.

Poetry, I love you,
but you will clearly ruin me.
Are you sure we can't negotiate,
have a standing transmission 9 to midnight,
if you'll give me the rest of the week?
Oh no—I hear her laughing again…

Iron Tag

life beneath Brooklyn, maple leaves,
foghorns and subway sounds fill the night,
sharpened sticks on concrete, stoopball and alleyways,
pensey pinkies, "hit the penny," playing iron tag right.

doo wop and shoop shoop on corners and the stoop
of a second floor walkup — small but bright
the view: a brick courtyard, crisscross of clotheslines,
socks and nightgowns sway, echoed voices rise.

an upward draft, aromas of diaspora:
soup of chicken, deli knishes of kasha
rotis, pasteles, arroz y gandules,
falafels, kabobs, and cardamom bryani.

swirls of the world over streets that speak
languages of promise: every mother to child
in corner luncheonettes and grocery stores
says, "stop touching the candy."

Rise

Imagine waking up,
knocking and hissing, you
could rise like steam,
straining pipes to the first, then second floor.
You could sputter multiple languages
and be called brilliant,
or you could just lie in bed,
look around the room in the dark,
unable to change your grainy swordfish night.
If all the hoopla seems to belong to others:
friends, laughter, children,
fun you missed,
maybe it's because your prime time
sits at the end of tomorrow's long afternoon.
When the pale sun rises,
one moment is all it takes
to use your treasure:
Rise!

Abby Lynn Bogomolny is the editor of *New to North America: Writing by US Immigrants, Their Children and Grandchildren* and the author of poetry collections *Nauseous in Paradise, Black of Moonlit Sea,* and *People Who Do Not Exist.* Her poetry has appeared in anthologies such as *Oakland Out Loud, In the Light of Peace,* and *The Freedom of New Beginnings;* journals such as *Quarry West, Porter Gulch Review, Sinister Wisdom;* and newspapers such as *The Santa Cruz Sentinel.* Originally from Brooklyn, NY, Abby founded Burning Bush Publications and juried its poetry prize for a decade. After serving as Faculty in English with Santa Rosa Junior College for many years, she continues to write and stir the cultural soup in Northern California.

www.abbypoetry.com